GREAT MYSTERIES

Water Monsters

OPPOSING VIEWPOINTS®

Look for these and other exciting *Great Mysteries: Opposing Viewpoints* books:

GREAT MYSTERIES

Water Monsters

OPPOSING VIEWPOINTS®

by Alan Garinger

Greenhaven Press, Inc.   P.O. Box 289009, San Diego, California 92198-0009

Library of Congress Cataloging-in-Publication Data

Garinger, Alan 1932-
    Water monsters : opposing viewpoints / by Alan Garinger.
       p. cm. — (Great mysteries)
    Includes bibliographical references and index.
    Summary: Explores the reports and evidence for the existence of mysterious large creatures allegedly living in certain lakes and rivers of the United States and Canada.
    ISBN 0-89908-087-1 (lib.)
    1. Sea monsters—United States—Juvenile literature. [1. Sea monsters.] I. Title. II. Series: Great mysteries (Greenhaven Press, Inc.)
GR105.G7   1991
001.9'44—dc20   91-15174

For Megan, Kelly, and Sergio

Contents

One

Water Monsters

Early one July morning in 1609, the French explorer Samuel de Champlain gazed over the surface of the lake that today bears his name. The morning mist clung to the water and swirled upward into the shrubs and trees on the steep shores at the water's edge. Suddenly the mirrored surface shattered with such turbulence that frothy waves formed and crashed against the rocky shore.

What Champlain saw was a *chaoussarou*, the mysterious creature described in the native folklore of the region. Though he saw it only momentarily, there was no question in his mind that the slithering, arching beast was a real animal. Further, it was much like the centuries-old legend described it.

Champlain's mysterious animal has been witnessed hundreds of times since then. It is by far the most frequently reported of the New World monsters. Still, experts disagree about whether "Champ" really exists—and, indeed, whether any other such creatures inhabit the waters of North America.

Mysterious Creatures Everywhere

While Champlain was the first European to see a lake monster in the New World, he certainly was not the last. As colonists and explorers moved in-

(opposite page) In this late nineteenth-century illustration, a sea serpent terrifies bathers off Pablo Beach, Florida.

This world map shows the Boreal Forest belt, the area in which almost all sightings of water monsters have been reported.

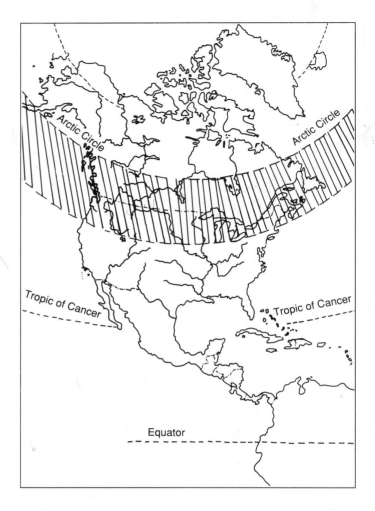

they found other lakes and other monsters. Recorded sightings have accumulated over the years. Today, at least thirty-eight states claim their own monster-infested lakes. Many states have several of them. Wisconsin holds the record. It has thirty-five lakes and one river in which monsters are said to live. Six Canadian provinces also claim many monster sightings. And at some time or another, a monster has been reported in every one of the Great Lakes.

The most commonly reported water monsters

are those long-necked creatures that appear to be cousins of the most famous of them all, the Loch Ness monster of Scotland. They are nearly always reported in deep, narrow lakes. These lakes are fairly young by standards of geologic time and have an abundance of plant and animal life that could support a large predator. They are well oxygenated and more often than not are connected by a series of rivers and streams to other bodies of water.

The Boreal Forest Belt

When the hundreds of reported sightings of monsters of this type are plotted on a map, all of them—"Nessie," the other European and Asiatic sightings, and the New World monsters—fall into a fairly narrow band of latitude. This stripe around the globe is known as the Boreal Forest belt. In North America it sweeps across the northern United States and southern Canada. Sometimes, because of

The Loch Ness monster of Scotland is undoubtedly the most famous water monster.

altitude, the stripe bulges north or south. This belt, then, could be thought of as "the land of monsters," because nearly all monster sightings are in lakes in this region.

Believers and those who study mysterious creatures are not surprised by this pattern. They claim the Boreal Forest latitudes are the perfect environment for serpents. Just as polar bears live in the northern latitudes, so do lake monsters feel most comfortable in the habitat provided by the Boreal Forest belt.

Common Traits

The creatures reportedly sighted in this region have several common characteristics. They are often described as brown to grayish-black and twelve to eighteen feet long (sometimes longer). They have long serpentine necks, rounded backs about two feet wide, and sawtooth fins running down their spines. Frequently reported is the great turbulence they cause when they surface. Yet they are usually described as shy animals that sink quietly into the water if disturbed.

While most common in the Boreal Forest belt, reports from other regions describe hundreds of unidentified animals that reportedly live in small lakes, rivers, swamps, estuaries, and bays. Some of those described have the long-necked, humped-backed characteristics common to those of the Boreal Forest serpents. For the most part, however, each habitat has its own beast that is different from any other. Once in awhile, someone will even report strange beings that are half human and half fish, usually said to be living in swamps.

Little Sound Evidence

While Native American folklore tells of many watery places around America that have legendary monsters, few modern sightings confirm their existence.

Researchers explain the rarity of modern monster sightings in several ways. For one thing, the small lakes and rivers that were isolated in former times are generally close to civilization today. If, as supposed, the animals are shy, they would be inclined to avoid populated areas.

Second, today these bodies of water are shallower and better known than they were even a century ago. Modern familiarity tends to diminish the mystery that surrounds even the more isolated deep northern lakes and rivers.

Even so, stories about monsters continue to creep into newspapers and magazines.

Anyone who lives in the continental United States is no more than 150 miles from a suspected monster habitat, and probably closer. Still, the probability of deliberately spotting a freshwater monster is small. They appear by unpredictable whim, as if to purposely confound the unsuspecting observer and thwart the scientist and the hopeful monster watcher. Of the dozens of expeditions organized to find a monster and the hundreds of watchers and scientists who seek them, none has ever succeeded in adequately documenting the existence of a single monster. But neither has anyone proved these mysterious creatures do not exist.

Reality or Imagination?

So, are the monsters that allegedly fill our lakes and streams real or imagined? One writer, Thomas G. Aylesworth says,

> The creatures may be real animals that we have yet to classify. Too many sensible, seafaring people have seen them and too many scientists are looking for them for us to say that they do not exist. . . . It is too early to reject the possibility that monsters do— or do not—exist. In the meantime, why don't we keep our eyes and minds open?

Another well-known writer on the subject,

"Except in a goblin world, to which I do not subscribe, there are no substantiated water monsters in the popular sense in American lakes. What cannot be disputed, however, is that reports of observations of unidentified aquatic or semi-aquatic animals have been and are being made with some regularity."

Roy P. Mackal, *Searching for Hidden Animals*

"That Lake Michigan is inhabited by a vast monster, part fish and part serpent, no longer admits to doubt."

Chicago Tribune, August 7, 1867

Daniel Cohen, wrote in *Monsters, Giants, and Little Men from Mars,*

> Freshwater monsters seem to be exceptionally good subjects for practical jokers. One well-publicized phony sighting will certainly inspire all other practical jokers or crackpots in the area, and one need not think in terms of elaborate conspiracy to explain how dozens and dozens of people can report seeing the same monster for decades when no such monster exists.

Many people believe that the monsters reported in the lakes and rivers do exist. Many of these only came reluctantly to accept this belief after having witnessed a monster themselves or having a close friend or relative who did.

Other people do not believe the animals exist. They blame active imaginations, superstition, and hysteria for creating the freshwater monster. According to this point of view, if witnesses have seen an animal at all, it is a very common one that has been misidentified.

Faced with a flood of reports by "reliable" witnesses, almost everyone admits that people are seeing *something that is unidentified.* Researchers are quick to add that "unidentified" means different things to different people. What might be unidentifiable to the average individual may be easily identified by a scientist. A witness, they say, might be an honest person and still be an unreliable witness when it comes to zoology.

Scientific Investigations

Since the question is not yet answered, most scientists adopt a "wait and see" attitude. The accumulation of information about sightings increases all the time. They hope one day to have enough evidence to know for certain whether or not water monsters exist.

Among the most eager investigators of these elusive creatures are cryptozoologists. The word *cryptozoologist* comes from the Greek words for "secret," "animal," and "science." Cryptozoologists study all manner of unexplained animals, which, of course, includes water monsters. Many cryptozoologists bring to their investigations knowledge of biology, geology, and other sciences. But in part because they focus their efforts on creatures about which myths abound but no hard evidence, many serious scientists consider cryptozoology a pseudo-science (false science). They disregard most of the information this field of study generates. As it stands, cryptozoology is viewed by many as primarily a hobby. Only those who write or lecture about these phenomena make a living doing it. And their findings remain controversial in the scientific community.

The controversy over water monsters continues. Whether lake monsters exist is not an easy question to answer. Nonetheless, it is difficult to imagine a person so dull and unimaginative that the mere mention of a sea monster brings no tingle of excitement and wonder.

"A formula constructed with sufficient complexity may fit a given phenomenon and yet prove nothing."

Winifred Wheeler, quoted in *Popular Archeology*, October 1972

"There is nothing wrong with not having all the answers at this stage of the game."

Loren Coleman, *Mysterious America*

Two

Champ

Samuel de Champlain had come to what is now New York state from Quebec, a settlement he had founded in 1608. He had set out with a war party of Hurons and Algonquins down the St. Lawrence and Richelieu rivers to Lake Champlain.

He was looking for the fabled Northwest Passage, an easy route for moving furs and other trade from the isolated regions of the New World to shipping points for Europe. The Indians in his company were looking for something entirely different: war with the Iroquois.

The conflict saw Champlain's friends victors over two hundred Iroquois braves. Horrified by the violence of the fighting and the torture of the enemy captives at the hands of his party, Champlain stayed near the lake long enough after the battles to make friends with the defeated Iroquois. It was during this stay that he saw the mysterious *chaoussarou*.

Champ Is Like Other Boreal Monsters

Champlain's monster sighting report has many things in common with recent reports of this beast, later nicknamed Champ. His report is also similar to reports from many other Boreal Forest lakes as well.

For one thing, Lake Champlain is a typical

(opposite page) Champ, the Lake Champlain water monster.

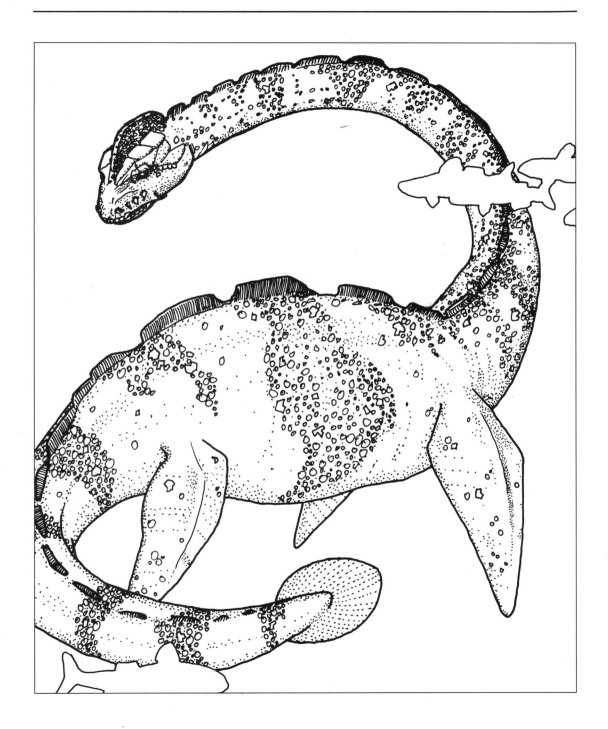

French explorer Samuel de Champlain was the first European to see a lake monster in the New World.

"monster lake." It is deep-shored. This means the water surface is far below the shore bordering the lake. The lake is deep. While it has an average depth of about sixty-four feet, in some places it is four hundred feet deep. The lake is 110 miles long, relatively narrow, and cold. These characteristics are typical of many of the Boreal Forest lakes.

Second, Champlain saw the creature in July, a prime time for monster viewing. Most of the sightings occur between late spring and early fall. Third, Champlain, like many modern witnesses, reported great turbulence when the creature surfaced. Finally, of course, there are the similarities in the descriptions of the monsters.

Like many monsters of legend, the *chaoussarou* was believed by the Iroquois to have mystical qualities. It could hypnotize observers, sending them into a trance. It appeared and disappeared, magically leaving only churning water as evidence it had been there. Iroquois holy men made charms of supposed *chaoussarou* bones to ward off evil spirits. In addition, ancient legends suggest that hordes of the creatures once frolicked in the lake. Today we would classify these stories as superstition. Still, the creature described in the Iroquois legends closely resembles what people claim to see today.

Two Schools of Thought

By the early nineteenth century, the settlement of the Lake Champlain area brought more people and, hence, more reported sightings. Two schools of thought had begun to develop. One believed Champ was real. This group was made up of those who claimed to have witnessed the phenomenon or believed those who had. The other group was skeptical. Some of its members suggested that anyone who saw the critter must either be imagining things or be intoxicated.

Champ's fame grew. In the early twentieth century, circus owner and promoter P. T. Barnum offered fifty thousand dollars, a huge sum for the day, for Champ's hide. Barnum, seeing the sideshow value in a sea serpent, wanted to cash in on its fame. Monster hunters came in droves seeking the Barnum prize. All went away disappointed. Yet the sightings continued. The 1930s and 1940s were prime observation years. In August of 1939, Champ reportedly chased a fishing boat to shore near Rouses Point, New York, before finally submerging. This sighting is unique because it pictures Champ as aggressive. Most often Champ and the other water monsters are portrayed as docile, shy creatures.

One of the closest encounters with Champ occurred in August 1947 when L. R. Jones and some friends were fishing off North Hero Island, Vermont. The lake was unusually calm. Suddenly an extraordinary eruption of its glasslike surface and a loud splashing sound at the north end of the island interrupted the evening silence.

"Out of the depths reared a huge dark form which moved swiftly in a northwesterly direction,"

Lake Champlain, home to the mysterious water monster Champ, is a typical "monster lake."

Sandra Mansi caught Champ on camera in 1977.

said Jones. "Three segments appeared, clearly discernable above the water's surface, separated one from the other by about five feet of water, the overall length of the creature being about twenty-five feet. It moved with incredible swiftness—about fifteen miles per hour—and disappeared altogether in about two minutes."

Sandra Mansi Photographs Champ

In 1977 Champ made his most notable appearance. Sandra Mansi, her husband-to-be, and her two children by a former marriage were having a picnic near St. Albans, Vermont. Once again, the lake was placid. Once again, Champ made his entry in a frothy uproar that sent waves crashing to the shore. To Mansi's surprise, what at first seemed to be a large mass of floating vegetation lifted a long curved neck and horselike head above the swirling water. Almost at once it swam swiftly away from shore.

Overcoming her fear long enough to reach for her camera, Mansi snapped the photograph that has become the best-known image of a New World monster.

At first, Mansi kept quiet about her adventure

Mansi snapped this well-known photograph of Champ at Lake Champlain.

for fear of being ridiculed. (It is likely that many sightings are never reported because the witnesses are shy about coming forward with the information.)

Then Mansi heard about Joseph Zarzynski, one of the country's most industrious and respected monster hunters. His interest and tireless work collecting and evaluating reported sightings of Champ has made monster watching more respectable.

Mansi's friends encouraged her to contact Zarzynski about her sighting and show him the photo. As a result, Mansi and her photograph of Champ became the highlight of a 1981 conference about the unexplained phenomena of Lake Champlain.

The possibility of a hoax always exists in things relating to monsters. Thus, scientists must meticulously investigate every bit of evidence that comes to their attention. A researcher from the University of Arizona, J. Richard Greenwell, carefully analyzed Mansi's photograph. He determined to his satisfaction that it is not a fake. It does show, he says, the image of a live animal.

Once Greenwell validated it, the photo was published in the *New York Times* and *Time* magazine, as well as in many books on the subject of unexplained animals. Discussion about lake monsters sooner or later gets around to the Mansi photo. It is the most compelling bit of evidence in favor of Champ's existence.

Daggerlike Teeth May Be Vital Clue

Sandra Mansi was not the last to have a close encounter with Champ. Reports of sightings continue to pour into Zarzynski's clearinghouse, Lake Champlain Phenomena Investigation. Nevertheless, many people are skeptical that Champ or any similar creature exists. Yet, faced with the growing volume of reported sightings, most of the skeptics agree that *something* is being seen. If not a sea serpent, what?

"The What-Is-It of Lake Champlain was again viewed near Barber's Point on Monday last. It was in full view of passengers aboard the steamer *Curlew*."

Temperance Advocate, St. Albans, Vermont, 1870

"Anyone who's seen that monster has been in the wine bottle. I've spent as much time on the lake as any living soul, and never saw a thing."

Roy Fleury, licensed Adirondack Mountain guide

"Silence from the unbiased scientific community may not be as colorful reading as the believers' tales, but is extremely significant. The fact remains that there is no solidly objective, scientific evidence that even suggests the existence of such creatures. Serious zoologists and marine biologists do not make a habit of confusing science and fantasy or calling speculation science."

Dick Sweterlitsch, dean of Graduate College, University of Vermont, Burlington

"I have never been able to understand why all things serious should have to be taken seriously; and, especially all the time."

Ivan Sanderson, noted cryptozoologist

Samuel de Champlain's first account of the creature may offer a clue. He said in his journal, "The fish had daggerlike teeth." Then he added, "The Indians gave me the head of it, which they prize highly, saying when they have a headache, they" draw blood by cutting the skin with the teeth of the fish "at the seat of the pain, which immediately goes away."

In this account, the word "fish" sticks in the mind. Did the Iroquois use the word *fish* to mean the same thing we mean today, or did they use it as a general term for anything that lives in water?

If they really meant "fish," there may be an explanation for what Champlain saw if it was not a serpent.

In Champlain's time, lake sturgeon were common in the cold lakes of the Boreal Forest belt. These huge, fierce-looking fish grew to enormous lengths. Their bodies were covered with large scales, and their heads tapered to a pointed nose. Their snapping mouths sported rows of daggerlike teeth.

Today sturgeon are rare and are considered an endangered species in Lake Champlain. However, Mark Abraham, fish and wildlife technician assigned to the lake, reports that even today sturgeon grow quite large. Sometimes they are seven feet long and weigh as much as 140 pounds. They sometimes gather in schools close to the surface of the water with their backs partially exposed. Several curved sturgeon backs could resemble a multi-humped water serpent. Additionally, their heads fit the description of the *chaoussarou* head the Iroquois gave Champlain.

Other Plausible Explanations?

Sturgeon do not fit all the evidence, however. No amount of imagination can make the Mansi photo look like a school of sturgeon.

If Champ is not a fish or a fantasy what other explanations can there be?

According to scientists, Mansi's photograph of Champ looks remarkably like the plesiosaur (pictured here), a large, prehistoric reptile.

The Mansi photo shows a remarkable similarity to what scientists believe the plesiosaur looked like. This was a large prehistoric reptile of the Mesozoic era, the time of the dinosaurs. Scientists believe the plesiosaur has been extinct for seventy million years. What a find it would be if Champ turns out to be one of these ancient creatures!

Another candidate is the zeuglodon, a primitive mammal related to modern whales. These animals are also thought to be extinct. Yet reports of strange whalelike animals still come across the desks of re-

This depiction of the Lake Champlain *chaoussarou* dates back to 1664.

searchers. Modern whales are creatures of the oceans, but they have been known to swim many miles up rivers and spend days, even months in freshwater surroundings. Thus, whalelike mammals, some researchers believe, could be the animals of the lakes.

A Giant Eel?

Ferry captain Gary McDonough crosses Lake Champlain several times each day. He does not think any of these explanations are correct. He suggests another possibility. He has seen giant eels in the lake. From his description, the huge snakelike fish are of a size that could certainly be mistaken for a lake serpent.

Larry Nashette is a Lake Champlain biologist with the Department of Environmental Conservation. A major portion of the work done by Nashette's department is the study of the lamprey eel population. Lampreys are parasitic eels that have infested many lakes. They migrate to the lakes by way of streams and decimate the population of more desirable fish. Nashette denies that an eel as large as the creatures reported by McDonough exists in the lake.

Nashette and his colleagues study eels using modern technology, including SIMRAD, a sonar device. SIMRAD produces underwater sound "pictures." None of the dozens of environmental technicians Nashette has worked with has ever encountered an eel as large as those described by McDonough. Their SIMRAD has not taken a picture of anything resembling Champ, and they have not seen Champ.

Champ's Hometown

Port Henry, New York, is the self-proclaimed home of Champ. If the number of sightings is the judge for this claim, Port Henry and nearby Bulwagga win hands down.

This relatively small section of Lake Champlain is the site of more reported sightings than anywhere else. A huge sign on the lakeshore lists the names of more than 130 people who claim to have seen Champ. (Samuel de Champlain is one of them.) The list grows each year.

Port Henry celebrates its serpentine citizen with an annual festival. Visitors can buy "champburgers" and Champ T-shirts, enjoy a parade featuring a Champ float, or browse through shops and booths that sell all manner of Champ memorabilia. During this summer event, Champ exists in good fun and laughter if not in reality.

Every spring as the monster season arrives, towns on both sides of the lake play host to a large number of monster seekers. Champ, whether it exists or not, is good business. Almost every Chamber of Commerce in the area refers to Champ in its tourist brochures. Mere mention in such an official document gives a kind of reality to Champ. It also infuriates the skeptics, who believe it prejudices serious research.

These same skeptics wonder: How could an animal of this reported size continue to hide in the lake and escape identification? Why has one never died, leaving its skeleton on the shore of the lake? If it is a mammal, how does it breathe when the lake freezes?

Champ Is Asset

When the glorious fall colors descend signaling the end of another monster season, certainly there are those among the thousands of tourists who hope to get a final glimpse of Champ. When this happens, even Champ's harshest critics must admit his "being" is a good-natured, whimsical addition to an already beautiful region of the United States.

Port Henry, New York, is the self-proclaimed home of Champ. Visitors hoping to catch a glimpse of the monster are welcomed by local businesses and tourist officials.

Three

The Pogo Clan

His mother was an earwig
His father was a whale
A little bit of head
And hardly any tail
And Ogopogo was his name.

from a British music hall song

Samuel de Champlain was mistaken if he thought his monster was the only one in the New World. The lakes of the Boreal Forest belt of North America allegedly teem with mysterious life. Perhaps none spur the imagination more than the Pogos of Canada. These mysterious animals all have "pogo" as part of their names: Ogopogo, Manipogo, and Igopogo.

Ogopogo reportedly lives in British Columbia's Lake Okanagan. Like Champ, Ogopogo exists in the legends of the early natives of the area. They called the creature Naitaka. Legend says the creature was originally a demon. It had possessed the murderer of a much loved old man named "Old Kan-He-Kan." As a memorial to this man, his people named the most beautiful lake in the valley Okanagan. Soon, the entire valley took this name.

The Indian gods changed the murderer into a lake serpent so he would forever be at the scene of his

(opposite page) In the depths of Lake Okanagan in British Columbia, Canada, the mysterious Ogopogo is said to reside.

crime and suffer there. The creature's name became N'ha-a-itk, or Naitaka, which means "lake demon."

Naitaka was a common subject for the art of these pre-Columbian tribes. Rock paintings (petroglyphs) in the Okanagan Valley show a fanciful serpentlike creature with horns and a beard. The stylized drawings appear in widely separated locations, yet they are easily recognizable as the same beast.

Naitaka is not as good natured as the legendary *chaoussarou* in Lake Champlain. The folklore describes a fearsome and violent monster. It delighted in devouring people who were fishing or wandering near the water's edge. Members of the Shushwap tribe were especially fearful and approached the lake with extreme caution.

According to one Shushwap folktale, a visiting chief named Timbasket ignored the warnings about

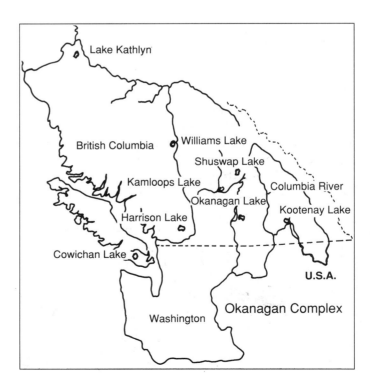

This map of the Okanagan complex shows the connecting systems of lakes and rivers. The arrows indicate the probable path of the Naitaka-like monsters, leading from the sea along the coast of British Columbia.

Naitaka. He and his family disappeared in the turbulence of the surfacing creature.

Because of Timbasket's fate and other incidents, the Shushwap developed the custom of taking a peace offering, a chicken or small animal, to drop into the lake's fearful waters. Many people continue this practice today. Most of them will vow they do not believe the "superstitious nonsense" about a lake monster. They will say they do it for the same reason people "knock on wood" or throw spilled salt over their shoulders—out of tradition rather than belief. Whatever the reason, they do it. So even today, Naitaka is a part of the Okanagan mystique.

Settlers' Stories

Settlers, mainly from England, started coming to the Okanagan Valley in the last half of the nineteenth century. At first they scoffed at the fear the Shushwap held for the lake. But soon they, too, became apprehensive. They were especially fearful of Monster's Island, which sits in the lake and where lay the supposed remains of the animals Naitaka had eaten.

The settlers, too, had experiences that added to the lake monster's bad reputation. People told, for example, of a settler who tied his horses to his boat to take them across a narrow inlet. Suddenly Naitaka struck, violently pulling the horses under the water. The terrified man frantically cut the reins, abandoning his horses to Naitaka and barely escaping death himself.

Stories of Naitaka found their way back to England, and monster talk became popular in the streets of London. In fact, it was in London that Naitaka got its new name. A popular music hall song whimsically referred to the monster as Ogopogo and the name stuck. All the other Pogos simply borrowed the last part of the name.

The reported similarities in Ogopogo's and Champ's appearances are striking and so are the

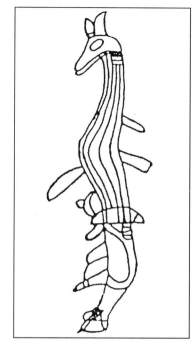

Native Americans originally believed that Naitaka, the lake serpent of Lake Okanagan, was a demon.

similarities in their lakes. Like Champlain, Okanagan is a long, deep lake. It is eighty miles long and eight hundred feet deep in places. Its shorelines are steep, forming the deep sides so common in lakes that are reputedly monster infested. (Unlike Lake Champlain, however, Okanagan never completely freezes over in the winter.)

Like Champ, Ogopogo is long-necked and hump-backed, but there are some differences in the animals as well. Ogopogo is often reported to have horns, a beard, and sometimes a mane. These characteristics make Ogopogo unique among the lake monsters. All the other monsters are described as hairless beasts.

A Carcass at Last

The most perplexing thing about freshwater monsters is that they are always alive. No one has ever seen a dead one. Logically, they must die and if they die in water, their bodies should float ashore. Where are the skeletons of these animals that supposedly inhabit the lakes, ask the skeptics.

Ogopogo, like Champ, has a long neck and a humped back. However, sightings often report that Ogopogo has horns, a beard, and even a mane.

Curious onlookers examine the body of a strange animal on the edge of Lake Okanagan. Was it Ogopogo, a manatee, or something else?

One day in 1914, monster believers thought they had the answer. The carcass of a strange animal washed up on a beach of Lake Okanagan.

The carcass was five or six feet long and weighed more than four hundred pounds. It had a round, flat head and almost no neck. It was steel gray and had flippers and a tail. This dead animal hardly fit the common description of Ogopogo, but many people thought it must be the mysterious lake monster. Certainly it was unlike any known Canadian species. Also, the blubbery mass was partially decomposed when it was discovered. Who knew what it had looked like when it was alive?

A local amateur naturalist, however, claimed the body was a dead manatee or a sea cow. How either of these animals could have come to its end in the lake is as great a mystery as Ogopogo itself. Neither lives within a thousand miles of Okanagan.

This questionable identification caused a flurry and inspired some people to believe that Ogopogo was, indeed, a sea cow. But this solution falls short

Have filmmakers really captured Ogopogo on camera?

of pleasing everyone.

In 1968 another important incident focused attention on Ogopogo. A man named Art Folden was returning from a vacation when he stopped on the shore of Lake Okanagan. He saw something in the water and ran to his car to get his movie camera. Stumbling across the beach, he made his way back to the water's edge. The footage he took has all the flaws expected in home movies. It is unsteady and often out of focus. But because it is a rare example of possible documentation of a lake monster, it has become a part of the mass of information referring to Ogopogo. It is mentioned in almost every book on the subject and was shown on the NBC television series "Unsolved Mysteries."

The Folden film shows an indefinable black blur moving in the water. Folden says, "The film shows a dark object diving and reappearing in a sequence of moves that indicates that it's moving out from shallow water into deeper water for a large dive into deeper water, then it did not reappear."

Researchers used the size of the trees pictured on the shore to determine the size of the moving object. They estimate that the figure was thirty to forty feet long.

In 1980, another Canadian, Larry Thal, was able to get more film footage of a mysterious creature in the lake. Thal saw what he believes was Ogopogo while he was on an outing with his family. He took several minutes of home movie film, which has been viewed time and time again by many researchers. While they say the film is authentic, they are not convinced it pictures a lake monster.

Arlene Gaal, an author and Ogopogo expert, pointed out the similarities between the two films. She says, "It's interesting that the animal that Art Folden shot and the animal Larry Thal shot are basically the same size. They are very large."

Another Ogopogo Sighting

In 1989, Ogopogo was sighted again. On July 18, Clem Chaplin saw something strange in the lake. He told his son Ken, who staked out the area the next day with a video camera. Ken Chaplin filmed the creature on the nineteenth and brought his teenage daughter back with him the next day. Both of them supposedly saw the beast, and Chaplin took some more footage of what he swears was Ogopogo.

The animal photographed by Chaplin was less than half the estimated size of those in the Folden and Thal films. This size difference increased the controversy about Ogopogo. Skeptics believe the Chaplin photos show an ordinary creature whose image is distorted by distance and angle. Many skeptics see a river otter or a beaver in the Chaplin film. They dismiss the films by Folden and Thal because they are of too poor quality to show anything clearly.

Ken Chaplin does not believe his film shows a beaver. He points out that the largest beavers in the Okanagan Valley reach about four feet from head to tail. He claims the animal he photographed was

"What Chaplin photographed was a beaver. . . . I've watched thousands of beavers. It was a beaver."

Mark Abraham, New York conservation officer

"For those who want to call it a beaver, I'll say, 'No way!' An otter? I can't buy it. That it's Ogopogo? In all probability."

Arlene Gaal, author and Ogopogo expert

much larger. His daughter described it as "about the length of a car."

He says, "I've asked myself a thousand times, 'Is there a possibility I could be mistaken?' and I just don't see where I could be."

Manipogo

Lake Winnipeg is halfway across the continent from Ogopogo and British Columbia. Lake Winnipeg is part of a lake complex that includes Lake Manitoba, Lake Winnipegosis, and Dauphin Lake. All these lakes are suspected lake serpent habitats. Of the reported serpents, Manipogo in Lake Winnipeg is the best known.

Manipogo is reported far less frequently than Ogopogo, but it still deserves a place in the Monster Hall of Fame. A 1962 photograph and the investigative work of Prof. James A. McLeod focused interest on Manipogo. McLeod is head of the Department of Zoology at the University of Manitoba. He has led several jaunts to the mysterious lake. His main purpose was to find remains of unidentified animals he believes might exist there.

McLeod's interest in unknown creatures stems from an unusual bone found in 1930 by a man named Oscar Frederickson. The bone was allegedly discovered along the north shore of Lake Winnipegosis. Unhappily, before its origin could be discovered, a fire destroyed it. Only a carved wooden model has ever been analyzed by scientists. Although a replica is hardly the kind of evidence scientists would put much faith in, the mystery of this unique bone eventually led McLeod to his interest in Manipogo.

Eyewitness Accounts

People fishing in the area reported seeing Manipogo several times in the late spring of 1962. Among the witnesses were Richard Vincent, John Konefell, and an unidentified American television personality who were fishing on August 12 of that year. They said,

> We first spotted the object to the left of our boat about three hundred yards away. After swinging into the direction it was heading, we saw what we believed to be a large black snake or eel . . . which was swimming with a ripple action. It was about a foot in girth, and about twelve feet of the monster was above water. No head was visible.

The photograph these men took is featured in many books on the subject of lake monsters.

Two things set Manipogo apart from the other reported lake monsters. One is the most unusual sighting anywhere in the annals of monster watching. In 1960, on Manipogo beach, seventeen witnesses said they saw a family of monsters. They reported seeing three—two large ones and a smaller one. This was the only time anyone has ever reported seeing more than one monster at a time.

Second, Manipogo is said to have a voice. It is described as an unearthly bellow, or sometimes as a sorrowful train whistle.

In 1960, seventeen people reported seeing a family of three monsters in the waters off Manipogo beach.

East of the Lake Winnipeg chain of lakes is Lake Simcoe, the alleged home of another long-necked, hump-backed monster, Igopogo. Lake Simcoe is different from many of the lakes that are supposed to be the homes of monsters. It lacks the long, narrow, and deep qualities of the others. It is, however, very close to Lake Huron. Some of the residents of Beavertown, Ontario, believe that Igopogo is really the monster frequently reported in Lake Huron, and it merely "vacations" in Lake Simcoe.

The Pogo Clan and Occam's Razor

What explains the Pogos and other similar lake monsters? Occam's razor is a frequently cited rule of science and philosophy. It states that the simplest of two or more explanations has the best chance of being true. This assumes that the conflicting theories consider all the facts. Here is an example. If a car quits running, the wise driver will check the gas tank before he or she tears apart the carburetor.

In the study of freshwater monsters, the absolute simplest explanation is that monsters do not exist at all. This, of course, is the skeptic's point of view. In order to take this stand, it is necessary to ignore reported sightings or reject them as unreliable or scientifically unfounded. Yet the reports come in such variety and from so many apparently reliable sources that they are difficult to simply dismiss. Thus in the case of freshwater monsters, a more complex theory is needed to account for all the facts.

The most common scientific explanations for the Pogos are the same as for the other freshwater monsters of the world: They are leftover plesiosaurs, misplaced zeuglodons, or misidentified common species. Yet these explanations fail to satisfy everyone.

Roy P. Mackal, author of *Searching for Hidden*

Author and researcher Roy P. Mackal believes that the water monsters of western Canada are actually sea creatures traveling far from their usual habitat.

Do sea monsters lurk beneath the tranquil waters of Lake Manitoba?

Animals, proposes a different theory. Mackal says the animals are creatures out of their usual habitat. They come from someplace else, perhaps an ocean many hundreds of miles away, and after awhile, return there. This theory has its beginning with Eskimo sightings of unidentified animals in the Pacific Ocean.

Could Ogopogo and sea creatures like the ones reported by Eskimos in the ocean be one and the same?

A Watery Network

Several researchers, Roy Mackal among them, point out that Canada's western region is an elaborate network of rivers and adjoining lakes. It is entirely reasonable, they say, to think that such creatures as those seen by the Eskimos migrate to the inland lakes and then back to the sea. The theory becomes even more believable when the reported sightings in the rivers and lakes that make up the

Okanagan system are plotted on a map. The points on the rivers where monsters have been sighted suggest a possible route, traveling by streams and rivers to interlocking lakes from the ocean to Okanagan.

Supporters of this theory became very excited in 1969 when a shrimp boat picked up a strange image on its sounding device. The *Mylark* was working in the Raspberry Strait off Kodiak, Alaska. This is the approximate location of several Eskimo sightings of strange beasts. The ship was also equipped with SIMRAD, the sophisticated sonic detector. The device drew the outline of a two hundred-foot-long dinosaurlike creature on the floor of the strait.

Of course, the monster drawing caused a great deal of interest in the migration theory. Soon, however, investigators began to suspect the image had been tampered with and that it may have been a hoax.

Those who believe in the migration theory say it could apply to eastern North America as well. All of the lakes cited as monster habitats are joined by lakes and streams to other bodies of water.

Many scientists think this theory is pure speculation. It would require the creatures to travel many miles through relatively narrow and shallow streams. People have lived near these waterways for thousands of years. They were the sites of Indian villages and are now the locations of modern cities. Surely the animals would have been sighted more frequently if they were traveling on such exposed routes, say the skeptics.

A far different theory is that monster sightings are the result of a type of mirage. Mirages are not just imaginary images seen only by people who are dying of thirst on a desert. In fact, they are quite common occurrences.

Everyone has seen shimmering patches of reflective air on the surface of hot pavement. Often,

"All it takes is a little atmospheric inversion, a lot of imagination, and you get a lake monster."

Skeptic from Berens River, Manitoba

"If what people are seeing is an illusion, why do they always see a weird monster? Why don't they ever see something else?"

Believer from Grand Rapids, Manitoba

This image could be the fin or tail of a water monster. It is, in fact, a log protruding from the icy waters of Lake Winnipeg.

images of cars or trees can be seen in these mirages caused by temperature differences.

The shifting of the layers of air, called temperature inversion, causes a "fool-the-eye" situation. Sometimes it produces a magnification. Other times sizes appear reduced.

It is like seeing a fish in the water. Because light behaves differently in the air than in the water, the fish is not where it appears to be. It is not even the size and shape it appears to be. The same thing happens when one looks through layers of air that have different refractive, or distorting, qualities. An observer unaware of this possibility could easily get confused about what he or she sees.

The lakes of the Boreal Forest belt are deep and cold, making an ideal setting for the conditions in which such temperature inversions could occur, thus causing monster-producing mirages. Relatively warm air swooping down the steep banks causes different layers of air to form above the cooler water. The possibility that monster sightings are a result of this kind of illusion has intrigued several researchers.

"If that isn't a monster, I'd like to know what the deuce it is."

Dr. James A. McLeod, referring to the Vincent-Konefell photo

"Many of the conditions under which lake monsters appear are ideal for the existence of strong atmospheric refraction."

W.H. Lehn, Department of Electrical Engineering, University of Manitoba

W.H. Lehn of the Department of Electrical Engineering at the University of Manitoba reported on his refraction experiments on Lake Winnipeg, the reported home of Manipogo. An article by Lehn appeared in *Science* magazine in July 1979. His article, "Atmospheric Refraction and Lake Monsters," describes the distortion due to a shimmering layer of air that accumulates at the surface of the water.

He says, "Many different shapes are reported for the monsters seen in any particular lake. This is not surprising if some of the sightings are indeed distorted and unrecognizable [sightings] of different though familiar objects. On the other hand, similar objects distorted in this way would also result in different descriptions."

He goes on to say that the motion associated with the sightings could be caused by the refractive effect. Objects in this condition would appear to move a great distance vertically even if the real shift were quite small.

Also, inanimate objects would appear to move when, in fact, they were quite stationary. As the layers rise and fall, there is often the illusion of motion.

W.H. Lehn found that certain weather conditions could make an ordinary log floating in Lake Winnipeg appear to be part of a living creature gliding through the water.

To prove his point, Lehn took a camera to Lake Winnipeg and photographed a log protruding from the ice. By careful attention to the qualities of refraction, he was able to get pictures of the log in which a very monsterlike image did appear to move. An untrained observer could easily be fooled by such a mirage. No one knows how many "reliable" reports can be explained by this phenomenon.

Lehn urges that future reported sightings include meteorological information. This would enable researchers to determine if the reports could have been affected by atmospheric conditions.

They Are What They Appear

Despite explanations such as those mentioned here, many people remain convinced that the Pogos are real animals. They have too many similarities, say the believers, to be anything other than what they appear to be.

Most of the characteristics reported for Ogopogo, Manipogo, and Igopogo apply to other reported Canadian monsters. The similarities in these descriptions leave little doubt: If they do exist, they are the same species.

If they do not exist, say believers, why do people thousands of miles apart report similar traits? The monsters depicted in the Native American drawings looked alike, too. Did the various native tribes across Canada compare notes before they made the rock drawings of their own special monsters?

Whatever the case may be, the mysterious beasts said to inhabit the Canadian lakes offer a lifetime of wonder and opportunity for speculation.

W.H. Lehn of the University of Manitoba conducted experiments to see whether atmospheric conditions could cause ordinary objects to look like water monsters.

Four

The Great Silver Lake Sea Serpent

Snake Daguerreotype
Perry, New York

M.N. Crocker would respectfully inform the citizens of Perry and surrounding country that he is fully prepared to daguerreotype men, women, children and even **SEA SERPENTS** over fifty feet long in the best possible manner.

From a promotional flier produced by M. N. Crocker in September 1855

Nestled in the Genesee Valley, about fifty miles southeast of Buffalo, New York, tiny Silver Lake is the home of one of the most celebrated freshwater monsters in North America.

Silver Lake is an unlikely spot for a monster. It is small—barely four miles long and less than a mile wide. It has neither the rugged sides nor the numerous inlets and bays that monsters reportedly prefer.

But the lake does have, like the other monster-infested lakes, a mysterious history in the folklore of the local Indian culture. Recent studies of Seneca legends indicate that Silver Lake was the summer home for several groups of Native Americans who for generations camped on its banks to fish and hunt. These people told of a monster that lived in the lake.

The monster described in the legend bears little

(opposite page) This illustration depicts the celebrated serpent of Silver Lake, New York, rising out of the waters before a crowd of astonished onlookers.

The citizens of Perry, New York, proudly display the image of the serpent on signs to their village.

resemblance to the fire-breathing dragon featured on the village signs of nearby Perry, New York. Seneca legends described the Silver Lake monster as a huge slug that was fond of the quiet serenity of the lake and became agitated only when humans did not behave with the same quiet dignity. Native Americans approached the lake in quiet reverence or not at all.

Friday the Thirteenth

The modern Silver Lake sea serpent made its appearance on Friday, the thirteenth of July, 1855. Four men and two boys were in a boat fishing. The sun had set and the lake mirrored the star-filled sky. Suddenly, just a few feet behind the boat, a long object appeared.

The fishermen paid no attention to it at first, thinking it was a log. Then it sank below the water and reappeared abruptly in another position, hissing and moving rapidly toward them.

Alphonse Scribner, one of the fishermen, tried to cut the anchor rope but dropped his knife into the water. Frantically, he pulled up the anchor by hand, and the men hastily tried to retreat to shore.

The "thing" submerged as the panic-stricken witnesses struggled with the oars. Moments later, it surfaced again at their stern just before they managed to beach the boat in a little cove.

In semi-shock, the witnesses made their way up the beach to an inn, the Walker House. After the ribbing and ridicule died down, the world heard the first description of the serpent.

Enormous, Fearsome Monster

The fishermen said it was enormous, with a body as big around as a flour barrel, which would make it larger around the middle than the clothes dryers in modern homes. According to the bewildered witnesses, its large, glowing red eyes were as big as dinner plates. It shot out spouts of water to the height of a small tree, and its bubbling and thrashing were as deafening as the torrent of water crashing at the bottom of nearby Genesee Falls.

The *Wyoming County Times* reported the incident on July 18: "Its head—it could no longer be called a log—was now within three rods of the boat [about fifty feet] and, as it approached, the waves parted on either side as if a boat were leisurely approaching."

The *Times* story continued,

All in the boat had a fair view of the creature and concur in representing it as a most horrid and repulsive looking monster. . . . On the opposite side of the boat, about a rod and a half [twenty-five feet] to the northeast, the other extremity of the serpent was in full view, lashing in the water with its tail. When the forward part descended upon the water it created waves that nearly capsized the boat and suspended regular operation of the oars.

An illustration of the Silver Lake serpent as depicted in a pamphlet describing the monster's 1855 appearances.

The very next night, another group of young men were taking a moonlight swim in the lake when they heard a sound "like a towline being raised from the water." Then the monster's hissing silhouette surfaced between the bathers and the moon.

This second sighting was too much for the locals to ignore. The people of Perry frantically organized a Vigilance Society. The group stationed heavily armed men at the lake day and night intent on capturing or killing the monster. The society also hired an experienced whaler, harpoons and all, to hunt the monster, but to no avail. The people of Perry built a tower on the north shore of the lake to give sentinels an unobstructed view. A group called the Experience Company provided one thousand dollars to help devise a means of capturing the creature. But all these efforts were in vain. The monster had gone into hiding.

Monster Mania

Then on July 27 it made another appearance. Ironically, it chose to show itself to Charles Hall, one of the original witnesses. Hall and his family were out on the lake when they saw the monster. One of the children later reported in an affidavit:

> All sat quietly in the boat and looked at it. It appeared to be of a dark color at first, but as it moved off going into the water, it was a lighter color, of a copper color. . . . Its head and forward part was above the water at least a yard, and upon its back it appeared to have a fin as wide as father's hand. . . . Its head was as much as fifteen or sixteen inches around and its back was much larger. . . . It [the head] was as large as a calf's head.

Rumors of the Silver Lake monster spread rapidly, creating a "monster mania." Amid the hysteria, a fifty-year-old Native American known as John John was interviewed and reminded the sightseers of the long-forgotten legend told by his people.

By the end of July, Perry was swamped with

visitors and thrill seekers. The *Times* even promised to publish a daily edition to keep the tourists up to date. The newspaper said in an editorial, the reports "have attracted to this village many of the citizens of the adjoining towns and villages, and quite a number of visitors have taken quarters with their friends or are located at Walker's well-kept hotel."

Business had never been better in Perry.

The monster displayed a talent for appearing during times when bad weather kept boats off the lake, and showing up briefly in isolated spots. Thus it avoided large crowds of potential witnesses.

Proof of the Silver Lake Monster?

On August 1, however, the monster was seen by at least a dozen different people in broad daylight. The witnesses did not know each other and their reports were taken as conclusive proof of the creature's existence. The *Times* said: "The existence of a monster fish or serpent species in the quiet waters

Perry's only hotel, the Walker House, was packed full of visitors eager to spot the Silver Lake serpent.

A.B. Walker, the proprietor of the Walker House, received an unexpected financial boost from the Silver Lake serpent.

of Silver Lake is established beyond reasonable doubt, if indeed there has been any room for doubt in the past week."

Newspapers across the country picked up the story and began publicizing the sightings. Many accounts noted that a monster had been "repeatedly seen during the past thirty years in Silver Lake." Reporters came in droves, as did a team of harpoon-carrying hunters, who constructed decoys of ducks and chickens in hopes of luring the monster out of hiding.

Other unexplained incidents were attributed to monster activity. A cow disappeared from a farm near the lake. Animal disappearances are not particularly uncommon, but since remains of the animal were not found, Perry citizens insisted that it had fallen prey to the monster in their lake.

Perry's only hotel, the Walker House, was packed to capacity. There was even a waiting list for reservations. A.B. Walker, the proprietor, had suffered a serious financial setback when the new railroad took away the business from the stagecoach line that stopped at the hotel, but the 1855 monster scare promised to reverse this trend.

More Sightings

On Wednesday, August 15, Edwin Fanning saw the monster along Chaplin's Landing at Silver Lake. His description fit exactly the previous ones, including the size, movements, and hissing sounds mentioned by the other witnesses.

A short time later, Joshua Jenks, who was heavily armed and out on the lake when the monster surfaced about fifteen feet from his boat, took a shot at it. Jenks was so excited he entirely missed the creature.

Author John Keel describes Silver Lake under seige in his book *Strange Creatures from Time and Space:*

While the searchers were clustered at one end of the lake, the serpent would suddenly bob up a mile away.

When bad weather lashed the lake and rendered small boats useless, the playful monster would rise up in the center as if to mock the teeming throngs on the shores. The perimeter of the lake must have looked like an army fortification, bristling with campers armed with bows and arrows, shotguns, rifles, and harpoons. One story even implies a cannon was either implaced, or was going to be, near one of the inlets where the creature had been seen most frequently.

The sightings decreased rapidly during the year and by the end of 1856, stopped altogether. However, this had no effect on the tourists who continued coming in hopes of seeing the now-famous monster.

A Telling Fire

Who can say how long the mystery of the Silver Lake monster might have continued had not the Walker House been destroyed by fire in 1857? Volunteer firefighters, digging through the rubble, were stunned by a perplexing discovery. In the attic they

This illustration depicts the Silver Lake monster being pursued by boatloads of eager "monster catchers."

found a huge, charred, suspicious-looking contraption. Further investigation proved it was the "sea serpent"—made of canvas over a wire frame. A. B. Walker left town and immediately headed for Canada, presumably just ahead of the vigilantes who were brandishing ropes and guns, intent on lynching him.

Walker is credited with creating the Silver Lake sea serpent. If he did, he accomplished a marvel of secrecy and conspiracy. Many details are still unknown. But it is pretty well established that the model was assembled in an abandoned tannery near the lake. This was no small construction job. How the conspirators kept from being discovered, no one knows. According to present-day photographer and historian Clark Rice, "It was the world's best kept secret before the atom bomb."

The canvas body was painted a deep green with bright yellow spots to give it a grotesque appear-

When the Walker House burned down in 1857, the Silver Lake monster was revealed as a hoax. Firefighters discovered the sea serpent, made of canvas over a wire frame, in the rubble of the hotel.

ance. The bright red eyes and mouth suggested a fearsome creature. A series of weights along the edge of the canvas caused the structure to sink into the water, and long ropes attached to strategic parts of the body allowed the conspirators to operate it like a gigantic marionette.

A large pair of bellows like those used in a blacksmith's shop were hidden in the basement of a shanty on the west edge of the lake. They were connected to the end of a gas pipe and extended into the lake by a small rubber hose. When the hose was attached to the framework under the canvas, air produced by the bellows caused the contraption to rise or fall in the water. Air escaping from under the canvas caused the turbulence and the hissing sound.

Description of the charred remains suggests it took at least four "puppeteers" to operate the monster. Three of them worked the ropes, and the fourth operated the bellows in the shanty. How did they communicate with each other? How did they choreograph each appearance of the serpent? When they were finished with their year-long performance, how did they transport such a large object more than a mile to the attic of the hotel, all the time avoiding the eyes of the townsfolk, the sentinels, and the tourists? Walker received all the blame for the publicity stunt, but who were his accomplices?

A Suspicious Photographer

One suspect is a photographer named M. N. Crocker. He traveled through the towns and villages in the area, making what money he could with his art.

Unhappily for him, his cart caught fire and burned in Perry. He purchased some land for a studio, but was deeply in debt. Obviously, an itinerant photographer had a lot to gain from a monster-inspired tourist trade. A favorite tourist item in Perry today is a postcard showing both the monster and Crocker with his camera.

One might even wonder about Charles Hall. After his first experience, it is strange that he would take his family to the place where he had days before experienced such a scare.

John John is another suspect. His story came at a terribly advantageous time. And John John did not tell the tourists about the "slug-like monster" of Native American folklore, but about a hissing and snorting sea serpent. Was John John a part of the plot or was he just "putting on" the white folks?

The origin of the legend is itself enigmatic. Robert Murphy operates the Sea Serpent Comics and Print Shop. He has done as much research as anyone into the legend and has produced several comic books about the monster. He believes the origin of the legend has more to do with parenting than superstition.

"Silver Lake was a temporary camp for the Indians who came here," he says. "They came to catch fish. I believe the early people told about the monster like a 'boogey man' story to keep the children quiet. Supposedly, the monster only became a threat if he was disturbed."

Could this also explain why later generations camped farther from the lake? Is it possible these children grew up believing what their parents told them and turned a harmless fairy tale into a fearful beast that became a legend?

There is an epilogue to the A. B. Walker part of the story. Eleven years after his flight to Canada, he returned to Perry. The townsfolk no longer thought of him as a scoundrel but a hero. During his absence, no matter how much the media denied the existence of a monster in Silver Lake, tourists came to see for themselves. They still do today.

An Important Story

The Silver Lake sea serpent story is important. It demonstrates how ready people are to accept monster stories. Hysteria is always a part of a sighting. And it points out that a hoax is always a possibility.

The Silver Lake monster hoax is also good fuel for skeptics. They can say, "See how little it takes to fool people? You float a piece of canvas around in a lake and all of a sudden there is a monster. And that 'Friday the 13th' stuff, how gullible can you get? And what about that disappearing cow? See how easily people make unsubstantiated assumptions when their thinking is clouded by a monster scare?" Skeptics point to the hysteria, the exploitation, and the hoax. If there is no real monster in Silver Lake, they say, there probably are no monsters other places except in the minds of people who create them.

Skeptics will also contend that the media were unreliable in 1855 and are little different today. Not only do they not get the facts straight about monsters, they have more to gain from a sensational story than they do from a humdrum one.

Visions Not "Just in the Head"

But for the believer, the Silver Lake story is refreshingly hopeful. Yes, it was a hoax. But it shows that people who claim to see something unusual often do. Their visions are not "just in the head." Those who reported the Silver Lake monster really did see something. Moreover, their descriptions were extremely accurate. They were not intoxicated, they were not imagining, they were not seeking publicity. The incident lends credibility to other sightings.

It may be too simple to say that there is not now —nor ever was—a sea serpent in Silver Lake. The sea serpent motif is ever-present. Perry has a claim to fame shared by few other towns. Proprietors of the Sea Serpent Inn in downtown Perry, New York, may say to guests, "We know it was a hoax, but it was a marvelous one!"

Five

The White River Monster

"I don't think there's any such thing," the skeptic said. "I seen a picture in the paper but I just imagine it's a big old gar [a kind of fish] or something. They've pulled gars out of the river that was nine feet long."

"My idea," the true believer said, "is that he's one of these here sea serpents that comes up here and spends the summer. I never heard tell of anybody seeing him except in the summer, so I figure he comes here to spawn or something."

"If he come here to spawn," the skeptic said, "that'd mean we'd have a whole gang of the things."

This bit of folklore is from the *Arkansas Gazette* of February 25, 1973. Columnist Bob Lancaster reported the conversation overheard at a filling station in Newport, Arkansas. Whether it was an actual conversation or the columnist's satire is unclear. Either way, it expresses some of the ideas the local people have about the monster that supposedly inhabits the White River.

Newport is the town that adopted Whitey, the White River monster. From time to time "Whitey" makes national and even international news. It is by far the most frequently reported river monster in the nation.

Bramblett Bateman's 1937 sighting of the White River monster is the most frequently cited.

(opposite page) Whitey, the most frequently reported river monster in the United States.

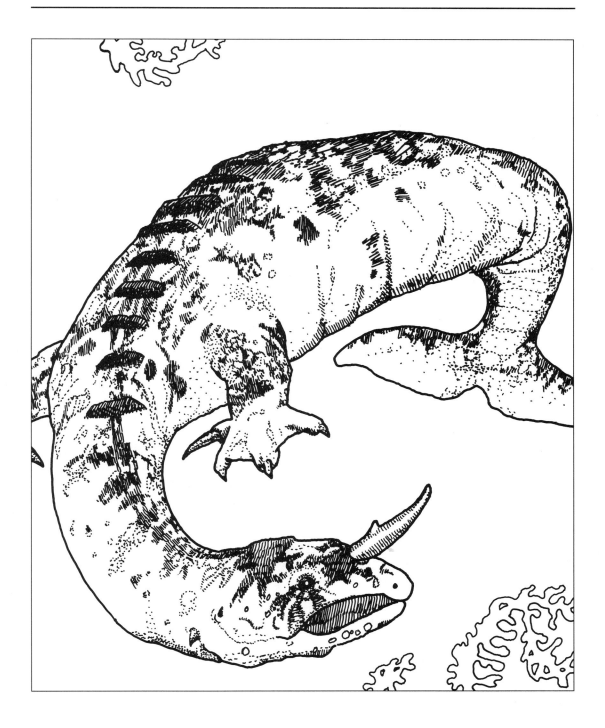

Bateman described in a sworn statement what he saw downstream from Newport. He said,

> I was standing somewhere near the east bank of said river. I saw something appear on the surface of the water. From the best I could tell, from the distance, it would be about twelve feet long and four or five feet wide. I did not see either head nor tail but it slowly rose to the surface and stayed in this position some five minutes.

Included with the affidavit was a statement from the official who accepted the report, stating that Bateman was a solid citizen.

A Second Sighting

Two weeks later Bateman claimed he saw the monster again. Also, he claimed at least twenty-five other people had seen the beast and would be willing to swear to it.

Bateman did not get his twenty-five, but three other people did follow Bateman's lead and filed affidavits. One of them was Bateman's wife. She said she did not actually see the beast, but she saw the "water boil up across the river about two feet high."

This turbulence is a common trait of nearly all the water monster reports. It appears, for example, in the statement of Z. B. Reid, a deputy sheriff of Jackson County, Arkansas.

When Bateman saw Reid's report, he called Reid and suggested they get together a hunting party to shoot the monster. Another deputy, Joe McCartney, accompanied them to the river where they waited for two hours without seeing anything. Finally, tired of the vigil, they were loading their gear into a car when a young boy shouted to them from the river.

Reid reported,

> We ran back to the bank and there was a lot of foam and bubbles coming up in a circle about thirty feet in diameter some three hundred feet from where we were standing. It did not come up there but appeared about three hundred feet upstream. It looked like a large sturgeon or catfish. It went down in about

two minutes. Joe McCartney started to shoot, but the gun he carried was not loaded.

> There is no doubt in my mind that it was something alive but I do not know what it was. We waited another hour but it did not appear again.

Reports such as these brought national attention to Whitey. By the end of the year, several people had come forward to say they had known about the monster for a long time. They apparently had been waiting for someone else to take the brunt of the ridicule before they were willing to admit to having such a bizarre experience. One of these late reporters was Ethel Smith of Little Rock.

A few days after Reid's encounter was reported, Smith said she had seen the monster thirteen years before. She claimed her husband and children had seen it, too.

Cryptozoologist Roy Mackal quoted Smith in his book *Searching for Hidden Animals*:

> The old highway ran right along the riverbank. My husband had stopped for some fishing when the children began yelling about the submarine in the

Whitey is often reported rising out of a mass of foam and bubbles, as if the river water was boiling.

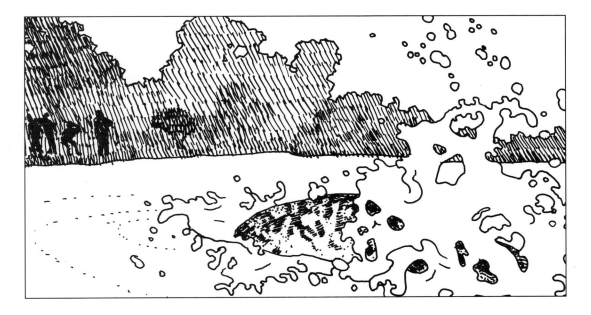

river. It was late afternoon and the thing stayed on top of the water about five minutes. It was making a loud blowing noise but never did show its head or tail. It was a terrible-looking thing with a dingy gray crusted hide. It frightened me badly.

As if not to be outdone in the I-saw-Whitey-first competition, George Mann, a White River fisherman, stated he had seen the same animal in 1915.

On July 22, 1937, all the stores in Newport closed their doors so the townspeople could go to the river to watch a remarkable event. While about four hundred citizens watched, V. W. Brown, a professional diver from Memphis, Tennessee, prepared to answer the Whitey question once and for all. He made several dives into the murky water with a harpoon, intending to capture the monster. But his attempts failed.

A few weeks after this attempt, a huge rope net forty feet by fifteen feet was manufactured in Newport to capture the beast. It did not work either.

Amazingly, the creature disappeared. After the flurry of sightings in 1937, there was almost total silence for thirty-four years. It was as if Whitey had taken up residence elsewhere, and gradually the people of Newport forgot all about it.

Whitey Returns

But in the spring of 1971, monster frenzy returned. Several sightings were reported in the Newport *Daily Independent*.

People were convinced that the Bateman creature had returned. Witnesses described "a creature the size of a boxcar," "the length of three or four pickup trucks," and "at least two yards across." Other characteristics were described: Whitey did not have scales. Its skin looked as if it were peeling, yet it was smooth. Many witnesses again reported the "boiling-up of the water" when the creature surfaced.

The report of Ernest Denks brought some new characteristics to light. He described the creature as

Ernest Denks reported that the White River monster had a long pointed bone in the center of its forehead.

being more animal than fish, and he estimated it must weigh about one thousand pounds. The most remarkable feature Denks reported was a long pointed bone protruding from the creature's forehead.

Cloyce Warren was most fortunate. Not only did he see the creature, but he also photographed it with his Polaroid camera on June 28, 1971. Copies of this photo appeared in newspapers around the country. Unfortunately, it did not reproduce well. The picture shows a barely discernable black bulge in the foamy surface of the river. People had only Warren's word that the object in the photo was an animal.

New Evidence

Gary Addington and Lloyd Hamilton also caught Whitey on film in a deep section of the river near Jacksonport. Unfortunately, the pictures did not solve the puzzle. They never made the pages of the newspapers or books about strange animals. They were ruined in developing!

Early in July, new information was added to the

Knowledge about Whitey increased when large, deep tracks were found amidst crushed vegetation on the river's edge.

knowledge about Whitey. Large tracks were discovered amid crushed vegetation on Towhead Island in the river. The reports said the tracks measured eight to fourteen inches and showed three toes with claws and large pads at the heel. Some tracks showed the suggestion of a spur attached at a right angle to the heel. Law enforcement officials made plaster casts of the prints, but little was said about the casts after they were made. Eventually, they were forgotten and no one knows what happened to them.

The closest encounter came on July 21 when woodsman and trapper Ollie Richardson and his teenage friend, Joey Dupree, decided to explore the river near Towhead Island.

As they approached the island, the water suddenly erupted. The men reported that their boat abruptly halted and then they were lifted out of the water on the back of a large animal.

The explorers were too shocked to observe what the creature looked like.

The reported sightings continued for the next three years, gaining worldwide notoriety for the beast. In one 1974 report, Leon Gibbs and Carl Jackson reported seeing two "things" swimming in the river. They reported that the mysterious things were "black and bigger than cows." After this, the reports dwindled.

Business Improves

By this time, however, the towns in the area were beginning to discover Whitey in another way. As has been seen before, water monsters are good business. Newport is the accepted home of Whitey, but nearby towns started getting into the act, too.

The White River Festival held in Batesville, Arkansas, started featuring Whitey themes. Thousands of people lined the streets as floats focused attention on the monster. If the monster was not real in the water, it became a reality on the shore and on the streets of the small towns near the river.

On February 16, 1973, the Arkansas state senate approved a resolution calling for the establishment of a "White River Monster Sanctuary and Refuge." The resolution sponsored by Sen. Robert Harvey made it "unlawful to molest, kill, trample or harm the White River Monster while in its native retreat."

The resolution states that the monster, "because of periodic sightings by reputable persons, has become a curious phenomenon and an attraction for both in-state and out-of-state tourists," and "it is in the best interest of the State of Arkansas to protect the now internationally famous White River Monster from harm and extinction because of the great tourist attraction." The resolution was reprinted in newspapers around the world.

A Japanese television network spent two weeks in Newport filming the river and interviewing witnesses. An independent producer spent weeks filming the White River. The *London Daily News* did a series of articles about Whitey. But none of these

"The White River case is a clear-cut instance of a known aquatic animal observed outside of its normal habitat or range and is therefore unidentified by the observers unfamiliar with the type."

Roy P. Mackal, *Searching for Hidden Animals*

"I'm very skeptical that there even is an animal in White River. I even knew the people who reported the first sighting in 1937 and I still don't believe it."

Mary Kunkel, lifelong resident of Newport

media people saw the creature.

What can explain the White River monster? Roy Mackal believes it is really an elephant seal. Many of the descriptions fit this animal. The reported size—six feet across and weighing about one thousand pounds—is right. The "splotched skin" is typical of elephant seals. The "voice" some Whitey witnesses attribute to the monster can be explained by the typical "trumpeting" of the seal. And the "bone" protruding from the animal's head can likewise be explained as the proboscis or snout of the mature male elephant seal.

The habits of this type of seal make this explanation even more appealing. While seals tend to live in tight-knit groups on land, at sea they become solitary wanderers. This is especially true of older males. It is possible that an elephant seal could wander hundreds of miles from the sea to take up residence in a freshwater river. It is not at all uncommon for seals to spend a portion of their lives in a freshwater environment. In fact, there is one species that is totally adapted for life in fresh water.

Finally, what about the reported footprints? Elephant seals are huge, heavy animals. If such an animal crawled out of the water on Towhead Island, it would certainly disturb the vegetation and leave enormous tracks.

What About Gars?

Even though so many of Whitey's reported characteristics fit the seal, a large group of Newport residents do not believe there is a mysterious or displaced animal at all. If it is a living thing, they say, it is just a school of gars. Gars are large primitive fish common in White River. They have large, rough scales and fierce-looking heads. Furthermore, they often swim in schools close to the surface with their backs exposed.

Another possible explanation is suggested by an incident that occurred about the time of Bateman's

1937 sighting. A certain W. J. Caldwell was fishing for catfish in the White River. His line began to tug so forcefully it nearly dragged him into the river. He ran along the bank, but even with the help of a friend he was unable to land his catch.

Caldwell's "monster" sped down the river where it became entangled in a fishing net. Before it could free itself, it washed ashore. Caldwell and some friends killed the "beast," which they identified as a 290-pound sea bass. A sea bass is not as exciting news as a monster. The Caldwell story was all but forgotten, and Bateman's monster stole the show.

Another explanation for Whitey is offered by the skeptics. They say that Whitey is not a living creature at all. It is a sunken barge that disappeared off Towhead Island in the early twentieth century. The water is fairly deep there—about sixty to seventy feet. These skeptics believe the barge periodically floats to the surface and then sinks again. The

Some people believe that Whitey is actually a sunken barge which periodically breaks the surface of the water and then disappears again.

frequently reported turbulence, they believe, is the result of the high winds common in the area.

Newport is a small town, less than ten thousand people. Everyone knows everyone else. While the newspapers are always careful to establish a witness's supposed reliability, the group of skeptics in Newport does not always agree with such judgments. This is especially true when it comes to talking about the footprints found and cast in plaster on Towhead Island. One Newport resident said, "They never said much about the plaster casts because they realized they were beaver tracks. Those early reports about their size were just exaggerations." More than one Newport resident thinks the prints were faked. Why anyone would invent such a hoax is unclear, but then, hoaxes surrounding water monster sightings are very common.

There are some other things to consider about the White River matter. Sightings of monsters tend to run in cycles. One sighting is reported and sev-

Some depictions of water monsters are more fanciful than others. This creature is half-man, half-fish.

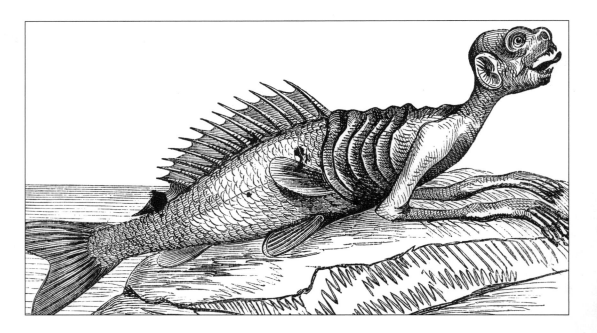

eral others follow immediately. The White River monster is a classic example of this phenomenon.

A rash of reports followed the first sighting in 1937. Then there was a three-decade dry spell. In 1971, the sightings resumed and interest reawakened. Now, more than two decades barren of sightings has passed. Is it simply hysteria that causes bursts of sightings, or is there a rhythm in nature that causes the animal to appear and disappear at widely spaced intervals?

People do not talk very much about Whitey any more. High school students never bring up the subject in biology classes. The high school biology teacher, new to Newport, does not even know about the monster. The only mention of Whitey in the news refers to the folklore of the monster and not to the monster itself.

A cartoonist may use the monster motif in a political cartoon to whip up support against the dredging of the river channel. An entrepreneur may print up some bumper stickers for a quick profit, but the mysterious animal that inspired this image is in hiding.

How long will it be before a new set of sightings starts another Whitey craze? If it happens again, will the people of Newport be able to settle the question of Whitey?

"Everyone knows about the monster or knows someone who tells a story about it."

William Harris, folklorist, Arkansas State University

"I never heard anything about a monster in White River."

Charlotte Jones, museum curator, Arkansas State University

Six

Some Other Baffling Monsters

Since legendary times, monsters have been reported in more than three hundred North American lakes and rivers. Some of the reports describe monsters with very unusual characteristics living in surprising places.

Consider this report from the *New York Times* on July 25, 1923. The scene of the observation was Alkali Lake in Nebraska, and the observer was a man named Arthur Johnson.

> In general appearance the animal was not unlike an alligator, except that the head was stubbier, and there seemed to be a projection like horn between the eyes and nostrils. The color seemed a dull gray or brown. There was a very distinctive and somewhat unpleasant odor noticeable for several minutes after the beast vanished into the water. We stood for several minutes after the animal had gone, hardly knowing what to do or say, when we noticed several hundred feet out from shore a considerable commotion in the water.
>
> Sure enough the animal came to the surface, floated there for a moment and then lashed the water with its tail, suddenly dived, and we saw no more of him.

Many other people claim to have seen a similar creature in the lake.

Alkali Lake, now called Walgren Lake, is listed

(opposite page) A depiction of the Alkali or Walgren Lake monster.

In 1923, five witnesses reported seeing the Alkali Lake monster.

in almost every mysterious animal book as being the home of a monster. Interestingly, this lake seems like an improbable home for a water monster.

Why Here?

Walgren Lake is located in the Sand Hills region of northwestern Nebraska near the town of Hay Springs. The lake is so small that water must be pumped into it during dry seasons. Otherwise, the lake would become too shallow, and would not be the popular fishing site it is.

Why would any monster choose to live there? No scientific evidence has emerged to answer this question.

Like many other water monsters, the Alkali Lake monster lived first in the legends of the nearby Native American tribes. The stories depicted it as a fearful beast. Supposedly, its appearance caused the earth to tremble and the skies to darken. It wandered the countryside devouring everything in its path. Later, when white settlers came to the region, they too were terrorized by the Alkali Lake monster. Reports said that it frightened settlers so badly they were "struck dumb" and their hair turned white overnight.

The last sighting of the monster was reported in the national media in 1923. An article in the *Hay Springs News* said five witnesses in different positions on the lake saw the beast appear. In part, the article said,

> M. O. New and Henry Wortman were the nearest. They viewed it from broad side, did not see its head or tail, color was brown, its back was eighteen to twenty inches out of the water, was apparently the shape of a huge fish, saw twelve or fifteen feet of body and think the animal must be twenty or more feet long.
>
> Jerry Hanks was possibly 250 yards away, saw it swim toward the center of the lake and disappear. Thinks it was a large catfish.
>
> William Hagedorn affirms that his attention was called to it by others, did not see the animal but did see the water splash as it disappeared. And he adds, "There is something there, and very large too or it could not splash water as it did."

Alternative Theories

Folklorists studying the phenomenon have an unusual theory about the characteristics attributed to Giganticus Brutervious, as the monster is sometimes humorously called. They point out that when the railroads were being built across Nebraska in the 1870s, many of the workers were Chinese. The horrible monster described in the legends is not unlike the common image of Chinese dragons. Some people wonder if Chinese tales influenced the image of the Alkali Lake legend.

Another interesting sidelight to this legend has to do with the report of an "overpowering odor" associated with the monster. Ironically, before Walgren Lake was called Alkali Lake, it was known as Stinker Lake. The chemicals absorbed in the water did indeed produce an overpowering stench. It seems obvious that the monster was unfairly blamed for the unpleasant odor.

The Boreal Forest belt dips south in the Rocky

"Despite the fact that not one of them has yet been captured physically, things like large, as yet uncaught animals in lakes and seas, and hairy ultraprimitive hominids, are, one feels, perfectly natural, normal and possible."

Ivan T. Sanderson, *Investigating the Unexplained*

"It seems safe to say, though, that any monster hunter can skip Walgren Lake, unless he's interested in bass or bluegill—pan size."

Joe Swatek, writer for *Nebraskaland Magazine*

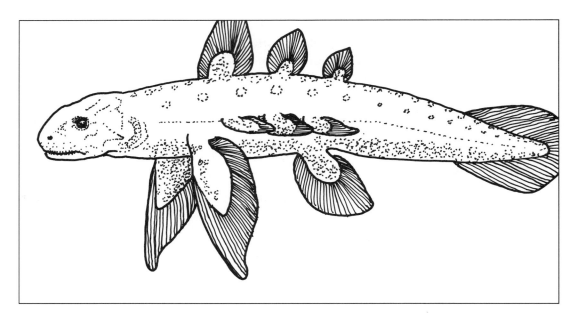

Slimey Slim of Lake Payette, Idaho.

Mountains to include parts of Idaho and Utah. Lake Payette in Idaho is the supposed home of Slimey Slim or, as it is sometimes called, Sharlie. (No one knows why this beast has two names.)

Lake Payette is a long narrow lake fed by mountain rivers. The modern sightings started in the 1930s and reached their peak in 1941. On July 2 of that year, thirty people reported seeing the monster, but no accounts survive describing what the witnesses saw. Weeks later, Thomas L. Rogers finally described what he and the others supposedly saw. He told a reporter, "The serpent was about fifty feet long and going five miles an hour with a sort of undulating movement. . . . His head, which resembles a stub-nosed crocodile, was eight inches above the water."

Rogers later said that maybe fifty feet was an exaggeration, but the beast was at least thirty-five feet long.

Perhaps the most detailed report is that of Mrs. Russell Brown. She was waiting for some friends to return from fishing. Standing on the shore, she saw what she thought was a log about one-and-a-half feet wide. But she said the "log" was steering a diagonal course and going very fast. Her account states,

> It was quite a shock, but I kept watching. There was a big protrusion above the water on the back of the exposed portion, which was about seven feet long, and there were three smaller protrusions along the side. I wanted to warn my sister, but all I could say was, "It's it! It's it!"
>
> People have tried to convince me that it was a sturgeon or some other fish, but that doesn't make sense, with those protrusions and all—and the color, green on the back and light underneath.
>
> I believe it's some prehistoric monster that's managed to survive in the depths of the lake. Oh, I don't mean this particular animal has lived all that time, there must have been at least a pair of them, and they may have young ones only once in a hundred years and these young ones live on and on— something like that, so that is the remnant, the last survivor, of a kind of sea serpent that is otherwise extinct.

What Is Sharlie?

Rick Just, author of *Idaho Snapshots*, claims to have an explanation for Sharlie. He says,

> I've seen Sharlie myself. At least many would have attributed what I saw to Sharlie. It was a stationary churning of water in Payette Lake that went on for about ten minutes. I also have a picture of it. My vantage point was excellent. There were no boats for miles and had not been for fifteen minutes. I don't know what it was, but I suspect some kind of change in normal lake currents caused by temperature differences.

So the question remains: Is there a monster in Payette Lake? Is it just a large fish or an unexplained turbulence?

Whether or not Slimey Slim (Sharlie) exists, its shaky history has led to its being subject to more ridicule than any of the other lake monsters. Jokes

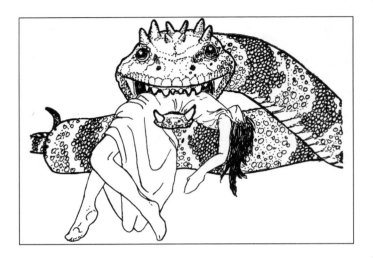

In 1868, Joseph Rich told how the Bear Lake monster carried off maidens in its powerful jaws.

circulated in the U.S. Senate and are recorded in the official proceedings of that governmental body. Many magazines, including *Time*, have carried humorous, tongue-in-cheek articles about Slimey Slim.

The Bear Lake Monster

Slimey Slim is not the only monster that supposedly lives in the Rocky Mountain lakes. At the extreme southeast corner of Idaho is Bear Lake, which Idaho shares with Utah. Bear Lake is also the home of another famous monster. For some reason this monster has never been given a nickname. It is called simply the Bear Lake monster.

Rick Just thinks this monster never existed. The legend started, he says, as a joke that went too far. In *Idaho Snapshots*, he tells of Joseph Rich, who owned a spa on Bear Lake. In 1868, Rich wrote to the *Deseret News* in Salt Lake City and told a story he claimed to have heard from the local Native Americans. It was about a serpentine monster that lived in the lake. It had stubby legs that enabled it to venture out on shore and carry off maidens in its frightful jaws.

Soon after the story's release in the *Deseret News*, reports came in from all over. It seems everyone was seeing the monster. Rich thought he should set the record straight. He wrote what he thought was a funny letter to the paper saying he was sorry that some people were skeptical about the beast.

He wrote, "I'm sorry they might come up here someday and through their disbelief, be thrown off their guard and gobbled up by the Water Devil. There are very few people even here, who disbelieve the monster." Rich went on to say the government would soon come to respect these people and relieve them of having to pay taxes. This last statement should have told everyone that Rich was joking.

Unhappily, people did not recognize the humor in Rich's letter. The existence of a monster in the lake became an established belief. It even made it into a scholarly report. In 1883, a group of journalists studying the Mormon culture came across stories of strange animals in Utah. One of the journalists wrote, "Bear Lake is pre-eminent for its mysterious reputation, inasmuch as there is abundant tes-

This depiction of the Bear Lake monster shows the characteristic hump-backed appearance of many water monsters.

Flathead Lake, Montana, is home to a monster who has made numerous appearances.

timony on record of the actual existence at the present day of an immense aquatic animal of some species yet unknown to science."

Once Bear Lake's reputation was established, reports continued to pour in. One writer was so convinced a monster existed that he encouraged the Smithsonian Institution to investigate it. The Smithsonian was not interested.

The stories persist. The lake has been studied by many scientists, but no one has been able to determine if there is—or ever was—a creature in the lake. Rick Just suggests that Joseph Rich contacted the *Deseret News* with the monster story just to stimulate business at his resort. If he did, his little publicity stunt has certainly had a long-term impact on the world of freshwater monster watching.

The Flathead Lake Monster

Almost every book about mysterious animals lists a monster in Flathead Lake in Montana. In 1963, a certain Ronald Nixon, who lives near the lake, saw "something at least twenty-five feet long and with enough substance to it as it moved near the surface [that] it threw a two-foot head wave. It

Children play around a model of the Bear Lake monster.

was perfectly black, and it didn't have a sign of any fin on the back. It couldn't have been a fish, and I'm sure it wasn't manmade."

Many other people have reported the "big black thing" in the lake. Paul Fugleberg, the former editor of the *Flathead Courier*, has collected many articles about the supposed monster. He has more than sixty well-documented reports in which more than one person witnessed the monster simultaneously. Fugleberg has offered a reward for the first actual photograph of the beast.

Elusive Evidence

One of the explanations commonly offered for this monster is that people are seeing a large sturgeon. Fugleberg agrees that a landlocked sturgeon is the most logical explanation. In 1960, a huge sturgeon was dragged from the lake, but there is some question about the authenticity of the catch. Many people believe that the fishermen were publicity seekers who hauled the fish to the lake in a tank truck and then "caught" it.

Some people believe that the Flathead Lake monster is really a sturgeon, the large fish pictured here.

"No scientific evidence supports the existence of a monster in Flathead Lake."

Craig Spencer, professor of biology, University of Montana Biological Research Station

"There are enough inconsistencies to give any conscientious researcher a severe headache. . . . That does not mean, however, that therefore monsters do not exist."

Loren Coleman, *Mysterious America*

Also in 1960, Fugleberg and some friends were aboard the cruise boat *Flathead*. One of the passengers excitedly pointed to a frothy patch of water on the surface of the otherwise placid lake. The passengers watched the turbulence expectantly, convinced they were getting a firsthand look at the monster. As the boat came around for a closer look, to their disappointment and embarrassment, the monster turned out to be a long line of waves high enough to cause undulating shadows. It was the shadowy effect that made them believe they were seeing an animal.

The University of Montana maintains a biological research station on the banks of the lake. Researchers there state that they have no scientific evidence to support the existence of a "monster" in the lake. They do say unusual wind patterns often combine with currents to create strange effects. Some researchers believe a partially submerged log in conjunction with these phenomena could fool a casual observer.

In spite of this view, the Flathead Lake monster continues to inspire the wonder of the monster watchers.

A Different Kind of Monster

Some lakes are homes to monsters that are certainly unusual but do have plausible explanations. Such is the case of Oscar, who appeared in Fulk's Lake located on the farm of Gale Harris near Churubusco, Indiana. Oscar is unique because no one speculates about the kind of creature it is. It is a turtle—a huge turtle—the "size of a dining room table."

On July 27, 1948, Ora Blue and Charley Wilson were fishing from a boat near the north end of the lake. They watched their bobbers as the dragonflies darted about the surface of the glistening lake. Suddenly a huge shape surfaced beside their boat. The fishermen recognized it at once as a turtle, but its back was larger than their boat. Its head, they reported, was larger than that of a four-year-old child.

Blue and Wilson watched in stunned disbelief for several minutes until the turtle quietly submerged. When they reported their experience, Oscar Fulk, the original owner of the lake, said he had seen the turtle fifty years before. The monster came to be called Oscar, presumably in honor of Fulk. Several other people reported seeing the turtle, then it disappeared for eight months.

Trapping Oscar

In March of 1949, a group of townspeople spotted the turtle again and were determined to capture it. According to one account, they actually did drive Oscar into a trap made of stakes and chicken wire. But the monster was too strong for the enclosure and quickly escaped.

The trapping attempt was filmed, and those who saw the film claimed to be able to see the turtle.

Oscar, the Churubusco turtle, evades capture by townsfolk.

Unfortunately, the film disappeared.

The trapping was reported in the local paper. The article was the first to report the turtle was "the size of a dining room table." This phrase was repeated over and over in articles written across the country.

Then it got crazy! A group in Cincinnati offered eighteen hundred dollars for Oscar. Hundreds of people made their way to Fulk's Lake to get a glimpse of the turtle. Cars lined up bumper to bumper one weekend. As many as four hundred cars an hour drove past the Harris farm. Many monster hunters brought tents and camped on the edge of the lake, hoping to see Oscar.

Harris turned down an offer by business people in Indianapolis to turn the farm into a resort. He had learned something from the offer, though, and started charging admission.

Documenting Oscar

The town of Syracuse, Indiana, the site of Lake Wawasee, threatened to bring a lawsuit against Harris. They claimed Oscar was really a resident of Wawasee and Harris had somehow lured the beast away from them.

Then the local turtle hunters went after Oscar in earnest. They decided to drain the lake to catch him. *Life* magazine sent photographer Mike Shea to record the hunt on film. Shea took nearly three hundred photos of the event, but none was ever deemed worthy of publication. Harris used two thousand gallons of gas in the pumping attempt. The lake was reduced to a soggy marsh, but Oscar was never seen.

Churubusco still calls itself Turtle City, U.S.A. Oscar is immortalized in festivals and publicity. A local Junior Achievement Corporation manufactures and markets a card game called "Oscar."

Few people in the area doubt there really was a turtle in Fulk's Lake. The size described exceeds by far any freshwater turtle ever studied. The closest

This cartoon of Oscar appears in a card game called, appropriately enough, "Oscar."

contender is the alligator turtle of the southeastern United States that holds the record for size, and it has never been known to reach the size of a dining room table.

Monster-Filled Waters

The lakes and bays of North America are wonderfully endowed with mysterious beasts. Some of them are reported frequently. Some, like Oogle-Boogles of Lake Waterton in Montana, are so rarely seen that no descriptions of the beasts are on record. One is frankly a myth. Saskipogo, which supposedly lives in Saskatchewan, Canada, has never been seen. Yet publicity materials describe it as a bizarre cross between a goldfish and a wombat. It turns out that Saskatchewan residents did not want theirs to be the only mainland province of Canada without a monster, so they dreamed up one. This last example demonstrates the fun monsters inspire in some people. Monster talk often takes the form of a joke or a light-hearted tale.

But for many, it is a serious subject.

It is not uncommon for people's attitudes about monsters to change. Paul Fugleberg states that when he first started writing about monsters he always did so in jest. But as he collected more and more reports, he began to take the matter more seriously. Both the number of reports and people's sincere belief in the monsters they describe convinced Fugleberg that monsters are indeed something to be taken seriously.

Seven

Looking Elsewhere for Monsters

Monster watching goes on and on. Do these mysterious and elusive creatures exist or not? Sightings continue to be reported in newspapers and on television. But at this time there is no conclusive proof either way.

In the absence of absolute proof, why do so many people believe they exist? And with the same meager evidence, why are so many people convinced that they do not exist?

Many scientists, anthropologists, and folklorists believe monsters are products of the mind. Some of them say there is something about the human mind that *wants* to see the weird, the strange, the fearful. They say this explains why giants, dragons, monsters with snakes for hair, and other frightening creatures populate myths and legends. It also explains why perceptions of the creatures may change with the people who tell the tales and the times in which they are told.

Regarding American water monsters, for example, the ones described in most Native American legends were violent, ferocious beasts to be avoided and appeased. Today, the monsters generally are thought to be shy, harmless, and innocent—if they exist at all. Many experts believe myths fulfill peo-

(opposite page) Whether fact or myth, water monsters continue to fascinate young and old alike.

ple's needs, and the myths change as people's needs change. So, for example, early Native American myths that showed the beasts to be ferocious monsters filled the need to explain disappearances and deaths that occurred on the local waters. They also served the function of keeping children away from dangerous areas. Today when many people are more skeptical of the unknown, the primary needs met by water monsters are the needs for fantasy and excitement. Also important is the economic need: Monsters attract tourists, which bring money to an area. Shy, gentle monsters provide the promise of a possible but not very dangerous thrill.

Monsters as Scapegoats

In 1948, an article about Oscar the Churubusco turtle appeared in the Fort Wayne, Indiana, *Journal Gazette*. It is titled, "Blame It on the Beast." In this story the author suggests that when things go wrong or when there are things no one understands, it helps if there is something "real" to blame. He sug-

While early water monsters were violent, ferocious beasts, today's monsters are thought to be mostly shy and harmless.

gests the "beast," or water monster, is invented to serve as a scapegoat.

Other experts agree. They say people seek a balance between the real and the unreal. When they cannot find this, they fabricate a "beast" to help explain the unexplained.

Some scientists conclude, therefore, that the real monster controversy is between the rational and the imaginative parts of the human mind. Dr. Gene Lykens, one of the most respected limnologists (scientists who study lakes) in the country, states without doubt that lake monsters do not exist. He knows of no evidence of any kind that would suggest the lakes of North America are monster infested. Yet in the face of his own scientific experience, Lykens still wants to believe the myth.

He is not the only one in the scientific community who does. Professionally, researchers may use their scientific skills to try to prove or disprove the existence of monsters. Secretly, many of them hope the mystery will not be solved. It would be like destroying the magic of Santa Claus.

If monsters exist only as a myth or mental contrivance, should people stop looking for scientific solutions to the mystery? Of course not! Myths are one of the most common starting places for scientific study because they provide the incentive for exploration of nature's mysteries. Many scientific discoveries have resulted from research into myths and superstitions.

Biased Data

Finding unbiased data on which to base scientific study of monsters is difficult. Most information about mysterious water monsters and other unknown creatures is found in newspaper and magazine articles. The coverage is balanced in favor of monsters. Dr. Earl Conn, head of the journalism department of Ball State University in Muncie, Indiana, explains how this happens. "If someone reports

"Nothing is rich but the inexhaustible wealth of nature. She shows only surfaces, but she is a million fathoms deep."

Ralph Waldo Emerson, nineteenth-century American philosopher

"Even when facts are available, most people seem to prefer the legend and refuse to believe the truth when it in any way dislodges the myth."

John Mason Brown, *Saturday Review*

a monster sighting, whether there is a monster or not, that is news." These stories add up over the years. As a result of these stories and already established legends, a body of water can get a reputation as a monster habitat. Once this expectation is raised, people who want to see monsters do see them.

There is no doubt that many sightings are made by people who are biased because they already believe a monster exists in a particular body of water. One documented incident is reported in *Nebraskaland Magazine*: "Two men from the state hatchery were stocking the lake [Lake Walgren] with fish. They heard a loud splashing noise nearby, but saw nothing. Ducks on the lake rose and landed restlessly, which the men interpreted to mean that the monster was feeding on ducks." Knowing the stories of the lake's alleged monster, the men reported they had seen it. Much later the truth came out. They really had seen only the ducks.

There are more immediate benefits to be derived from monster watching that have little to do

An illustration of the monster of Lake Utopia, New Brunswick, Canada.

with finding monsters. Joseph Zarzynski has kept a vigil on Lake Champlain for years. His interest is, of course, Champ. But in his efforts to protect his favorite monster, he has coincidentally provided another service. He has become a watchdog of environmental practices in the lake.

Zarzynski constantly corresponds with the New York Department of Environmental Conservation, because he is afraid that chemicals used to kill lamprey eels will also harm Champ. His interest in monsters has made other people more aware of all forms of life in the lake.

This is important in all our waterways. The lakes and rivers of our country are in danger of becoming so polluted that nothing can live in them. That, of course, includes monsters. Monster watchers are in a good position to observe the general health of the watery environment. They may never see a monster, but they can be a driving force to save the lakes in which monsters allegedly live.

Fascination with Mysterious Monsters Continues

There is little danger that monster mania will cease. Towns and cities near monster sites across North America will keep the legends strong. The media will continue to cover monster sightings because they make good stories. People with curious minds will go on seeking answers.

Monsters afford a fascination with the unknown—a sense of mystery without which life would be dreary. It is *mystery* that captivates people. Perhaps the major reason people seek solutions to mysteries is that they know each solution brings with it more mysteries to tantalize them.

Appendix A

Lake and River Monsters of North America

USA MONSTERS

Alaska
  Big Lake
  Crosswinds Lake
  Lake Illamna
  Kalooluk Lake
  Lake Minchumina
  Nonvianuk Lake
Arkansas
  Bedias Creek
  Lake Conway
  Illinois River
  Mud Lake
  White River
California
  Elizabeth Lake
  Lake Elsinore
  Lake Folsom
  Homer Lake
  Lafayette Lake
  Lake Tahoe
Colorado
  Lake Como
Connecticut
  Basile Lake
  Connecticut River
Florida
  Lake Clinch
  Lake Monroe
  North Fork St. Lucie River
  St. John's River
  Suwannee River
Georgia
  Chattahoochee River
  No Man's Friend Pond
  Savannah River

  Smith Lake
Idaho
  Lake Coeur d'Alene
  Lake Payette
  Pend Oreille Lake
  Snake River
  Tautphaus Park Lake
Illinois
  Four Lakes Village Lake
  Lake Michigan
  Stump Pond
  Thompson's Lake
Indiana
  Bass Lake
  Big Chapman Lake
  Eagle Lake
  Hollow Block Lake
  Huntington's Lake
  Lake Manitou (Devil's Lake)
  Lake Maxinkuckee
  Lake Michigan
  Wabash River
Iowa
  Spirit Lake
Kansas
  Kingman County Lake
Kentucky
  Herrington Lake
  Ohio River
  Reynolds Lake
Louisiana
  Calcasieu River
Maine
  Boyden Lake
  Chain Lakes
  Machias Lake
  Moosehead Lake

Rangely Lake
Sysladobsis Lake
Massachusetts
Twin Lakes
Silver Lake
Michigan
Au Train Lake
Basswood Lake
Lake Huron
Lake Michigan
Narrow Lake
Paint River
Lake Superior
Swan Lake
Minnesota
Big (or Great) Sandy Lake
Mississippi
Mississippi River
Pascagoula River
Missouri
Lake Creve Coeur
Kansas River
Mississippi River
Missouri River
Lake of the Ozarks
Montana
Flathead Lake
Missouri River
Waterton Lake
Nebraska
Alkali Lake (renamed Walgren Lake)
Missouri River
Nevada
Lake Mead
Pegrand Lake
Pyramid Lake
New Jersey
North Shrewsbury River
Passaic Falls
New York
Baldwinsville Mill Pond
Black River
Canandaigua Lake
Lake Champlain
Lake George
Hudson River

McGuire's Pond
Lake Onondaga
Lake Ontario
Silver Lake
Spirit Lake
Wading River
Lake of the Woods
North Carolina
Little Tennessee River
Valley River
North Dakota
Devil's Lake
Ohio
Lake Erie
Olentangy River
Slaven's Pond
Oregon
Crater Lake
Crescent Lake
Forked Mountain Lake
Hollow Block Lake
Upper Klamath Lake
Wallowa Lake
Pennsylvania
Wolf Pond
South Carolina
Goose Creek Lagoon
South Dakota
Campbell Lake
Texas
Brazos River
Klamath Lake
Utah
Bear Lake
Great Salt Lake
Mud Lake
Sevier Lake
Utah Lake
Vermont
Lake Champlain
Connecticut River
Dead Creek
Lake Memphremagog
Winooski River
Washington
Chelan Lake

Omak Lake
Quinault Lake
Rock Lake
Lake Washington
Wisconsin
  Brown's Lake
  Chippewa Lake
  Devil's Lake
  Elkhart Lake
  Fowler Lake
  Lake Geneva
  Madison Four Lakes
  Mendota Lake
  Mississippi River
  Lake Monova
  Pewaukee Lake
  Red Cedar Lake and River
  Rock Lake
  Lake Superior
  Lake Waubeau
  Lake Winnebago
  Yellow River
Wyoming
  Lake DeSmet
  Hutton Lake
  Lake Katherine
  Lake La Metrie

CANADIAN MONSTERS

Alberta
  Battle River
  North Saskatchewan River
British Columbia
  Campbell River
  Lake Cowichan
  Harrison Lake
  Lake Okanagan
  Seton Lake
  Sushwap Lake
  Thetis Lake
  Lake Tagai
Manitoba
  Cedar Lake

Lake Dauphin
Dirty Water Lake
Lake Manitoba
Lake Winnipeg
Lake Winnipegosis
New Brunswick
  Skiff Lake
  Lake Utopia
Ontario
  Lake of Bays
  Berens Lake
  Deschenes Lake
  Mazinaw Lake
  Muskrat Lake
  Lake Ontario
  Ottawa River
  Lake Simcoe
Quebec
  Lac Aylmer
  Lac Baskatong
  Blue Sea Lake
  Lake Champlain
  Reservoir Gouin
  Lac Massawippi
  Lac Mekinac
  Lac Memphremagog
  Mocking Lake
  Lac-des-Piles
  Lac Pohengamok
  Lac Remi
  Lac St. Clair
  Lac St. Francios
  Lac St. Jean
  Lac-a-la-Tortue
  Les-Trois-Lac
  Lake Williams

Appendix B
Organizations to Contact

Here is a list of sources of material about the monsters discussed in this book. For the most part the material is free, but many of the agencies ask for a self-addressed stamped envelope (SASE) with each request.

Alkali Lake Monster
Nebraska Game and Parks Commission
220 North 23rd Street
P.O. Box 30370
Lincoln, NE 68503
(Send SASE)

Churubusco Turtle
Churubusco Chamber of Commerce
P.O. Box 83
Churubusco, IN 46723

Lake Champlain Monster
The Lake Champlain Regional Chamber of Commerce
209 Battery Street
P.O. Box 453
Burlington, VT 05402-0453

Champ Channels Newsletter
The Lake Champlain Phenomena Investigation
P.O. Box 2134
Wilton, NY 12866

Moriah Chamber of Commerce
Port Henry, NY 12974
(Send SASE)

Feinberg Library
State University of New York at Plattsburg
Plattsburg, NY 12901
(charges for photocopies)

Ogopogo

The Okanagan-Similkameen Pentincton Chamber of
Commerce
185 Lakeshore Drive
Pentincton, BC V2A 1B7 Canada

Kelowna Chamber of Commerce
544 Hardy Avenue
Kelowna, BC V1Y 6C9 Canada

Silver Lake Monster

Town Hall
P.O. Box 205
Perry, NY 14530
(Send SASE)

Slimey Slim and Bear Lake Monsters

Idaho Department of Parks and Recreation
State House Mail
Boise, ID 83720

White River Monster

Newport Chamber of Commerce
210 Elm Street
P.O. Box 518
Newport, AR 72112
(Send SASE)

For Further Exploration

Thomas G. Aylesworth, *Science Looks at Mysterious Monsters*. New York: Julian Messner, 1983.

Daniel Cohen, *A Modern Look at Monsters*. New York: Dodd, Mead & Company, 1970.

Daniel Cohen, *Monsters, Giants, and Little Men from Mars*. Garden City, NY: Doubleday, 1975.

Loren Coleman, *Curious Encounters*. Winchester, MA: Faber & Faber, Inc., 1985.

Loren Coleman, *Mysterious America*. Winchester, MA: Faber & Faber, Inc., 1983.

Peter Costello, *In Search of Lake Monsters*. New York: Coward, McCann & Geoghegan, 1974.

George M. Eberhart, *Monsters*. New York & London: Garland Publishing, Inc., 1983.

Charles H. Fort, *The Books of Charles Fort*. New York: Henry Holt and Company, 1941.

John A. Keel, *Strange Creatures from Time and Space*. Greenwich, CT: Fawcett Publications, 1978.

Alan Landsburg, *In Search of* . . . . New York: Everest House, 1978.

W.H. Lehn, "Atmospheric Refraction and Lake Monsters," *Science*, July 13, 1979.

Roy P. Mackal, *Searching for Hidden Animals*. Garden City, NY: Doubleday & Company, Inc., 1980.

Roy P. Mackal, *The Monsters of Loch Ness*. Chicago, IL: The Swallow Press, 1976.

Reader's Digest, *Mysteries of the Unexplained*. Pleasantville, NY: The Reader's Digest Association, Inc., 1982.

Ivan T. Sanderson, *Investigating the Unexplained*. Englewood Cliffs, NJ: Prentice-Hall, Inc., 1972.

Ivan T. Sanderson, *Things*. New York: Pyramid Books, 1967.

Index

About the Author

Alan Garinger writes primarily for the educational media: television, computer courseware, and the print material that supports the electronic components. His specialty is adult education. He has written forty-five half-hour instructional TV programs that are broadcast nationally on PBS and commercial stations. In the past six years he has completed nine adult education "tele-text" books that accompany these TV broadcasts. In 1986, Garinger wrote an award-winning one-hour PBS special, "A Good Beginning Has No End." It was seen nationally on PBS stations.

The author, a native Hoosier and graduate of Ball State University in Muncie, Indiana, spent twenty-seven years in education, teaching at every level from kindergarten to college. In 1966 he received Indiana's Outstanding Educator award. He has been an elementary school principal and a director of community programs.

A full-time free-lance writer since 1984, he is a co-director of Midwest Writers, a group that provides educational services to aspiring and beginning writers. He is a frequent speaker and instructor at writer seminars.

Picture Credits